Ready to Change My Name

*A Spiritual Journey
from FEAR
to FAITH*

Third Edition

Gail E. Dudley

Cover Design

Shelbi T. Harris
Shel 10, LLC
www.Shel10.com

Copyediting and Interior Page Formatting

Kathy Curtis
www.christianbookformat.com
christianbookformat@gmail.com

Published by Gail E. Dudley
www.GailDudley.com
Highly Recommended International, Inc.
Ministry In Motion Ministries International
The Church at North Pointe
www.GetRealLife.net
Columbus, Ohio
United States of America
614-441-8178
e-mail: GED@MIMToday.org

Melissa

I pray this blesses
you as you embark
on this next stage
of your journey!

Love you lots,

Madenn

♡

DEDICATION

Romans 12:1-2 speaks to us clearly and with great power what the Lord desires for our lives:

"Therefore, I urge you brothers in view of God's mercy, to offer your bodies as living sacrifices, holy and pleasing to God – this is your spiritual act of worship. Do not conform any longer to the pattern of this world, but be transformed by the renewing of your mind. Then you will be able to test and approve what God's will is – his good, pleasing and perfect will."

I dedicate this book to every person who is lost, lonely, seeking significance, and who has a desire to become whole. I encourage you to begin the transformation process and give of yourselves as a living sacrifice, holy and pleasing to God. Let us begin by laying down the masks; removing the many masks you may wear depending upon the day or the hour, searching yourself with truth and honesty, and becoming a faithful believer in Christ Jesus. I pray from this day forward that you will step out in faith and live as God, our Father in Heaven, has ordained for you to live.

In Obedience to Christ,

ACKNOWLEDGMENTS

I worship and adore You, El-Elyon, the Most High God! I bless Your name, Jehovah-Nissi. You are my Victory. Thank You, God, for saving me. Thank You, God, for allowing me by Your grace to be the vessel to reach hurting people through this book.

To my pastor, husband, best friend, and the priest of our home, The Reverend Dr. Kevin Dudley, I love you. Thank you for believing in me when I did not believe in myself. Thank you for teaching me how to face the life of ministry with power.

To my children, Alexander and Dominiq, I praise God for you! I love it when I hear you say, "My mom is cool." Share with others that it's "cool" to be a Christian because you see it firsthand.

To my parents and my late "Papa," thank you for loving me. I'm fortunate to have parents who are proud of their children.

God bless you, Brenda Troy! You are a powerful woman of God. I love and appreciate you. And to Stephanie Thomas, I praise God that He allowed our paths to cross.

Ministry in Motion Int'l, partners: Thank you for always supporting and encouraging me to utilize the gifts that God has placed within me. To the ministry partners of our church, thank you for allowing me to be me.

To Attorney Evelyn Robinson, thanks for your expert legal counsel.

A special thank you to Shelbi T. Harris, a truly gifted graphic artist who designed the newest edition book cover.

To Susan Mackey, I appreciate the time and assistance you gave as I prepared this book for the editor. May God richly bless my editor, Kathy Curtis. I appreciate your time and dedication.

To the Body of Christ, be blessed.

FOREWORD

How truly blessed we are by the grace of God to have been given abundant and eternal life through Jesus Christ. Our lives are constantly being unfolded to reveal our place of purpose, peace, and power within the Lord's redemptive plan. Yet we inevitably face along this life's journey much that seeks to interfere with our growth, frustrate our prosperity, and impede our forward motion. Without the necessary tools that permit our victory in Christ to be translated to victory in our daily living and relationships, we end up being accomplices to our own injury.

I appreciate and applaud the work of Pastor Gail Dudley, my wife and friend of many years. She has a unique way of being able to minister to people of faith through her own life's journey by the gift of her words. One has but to be exposed to her irresistible style of relevant teaching, endearing personality, and remarkable insight for only a short time before sensing the very hand of God at work. In this book are tools to help all people of faith realize their God-given potential by finding the courage to face themselves as they share in the story of Naomi, Ruth, and Orpah. With biblical integrity, sensitivity to the Spirit of God, and concern for personal growth, Gail offers the challenge to us to be "real" and ever "ready to change our name."

The Reverend Dr. Kevin R. Dudley
Senior Pastor, The Church at North Pointe, Columbus, OH

Contents

INTRODUCTION

It is not by mistake that you hold in your hands a copy of this book. Therefore, I invite you to walk with me as I take you down a road often traveled.

Imagine traveling down a road with two of your friends whom you have called family and whom you love dearly, leaving a place that you have called home for many years. You are leaving the place where you have spent much time, shared your gifts and talents, and lived through some tough times. You are on your way to a place that is unfamiliar to you. While traveling, one of your friends turns to you and says, "Go back — to the place that is familiar. I pray that the Lord will bless you for the thought of going with me, you're so kind, thank you; but return to the place that you call home." With tears you turn to your friend and say, *"I'll go with you."* You've been with this friend half of your life. You love her dearly and deep inside you want to show love and compassion. Just as you set out to continue your journey, there is a voice inside of you saying, *"Go back to the place that you call home."* You decide to travel with your friends for a little while longer. There's a reoccurring voice calling out to you, "Go back to the rich and prosperous land that you believe to be true even today." What do you do?

Meet Orpah. She is the woman that set off on a journey with her mother-in-law and sister-in-law, headed to the land of Judah. Naomi, the mother-in-law, turned to Orpah and Orpah's sister-in-law, Ruth, encouraging them to turn away and head to their homeland. Eventually, Orpah wept, kissed her mother-in-law good-bye, and began her journey back to her homeland. However, Ruth, her sister-in-law, clung to their mother-in-law. Even after Naomi pointed out to Ruth that Orpah was going back to her people and her gods, Ruth took the stand to stay with Naomi and travel with her to her land. Naomi tried over and over again to get Ruth to turn back with Orpah. However, Ruth replied, "Don't urge me to leave you or to turn back from you. Where you go I will go, and where you stay I will stay. Your people will be my people and your God my God." (Ruth 1:16)

As I looked deep into this passage of Scripture, God spoke to me asking me my thoughts of Orpah. Forced to dig deep into my own life, I began to ask the questions, *"Why did she turn back?" "Was she unhappy with herself?" "Was she afraid of something?" "Was she unhappy with life in general?" "Did she run away from a situation that she felt she could not handle?"* While pondering these questions and many others, God asked me if I saw myself in Orpah. Orpah wanted to return to Moab, a place she believed to be "rich and prosperous," a place where she would be with her people and her gods. Studying this text and praying and meditating on this scene, I began to see the correlation between Orpah and myself. It was at that moment I realized my name was not only Gail Dudley, but that I had some characteristics of Orpah in me. Is it possible that all of us have some characteristics of Orpah on the inside of us? Could my name be Orpah? Is your name Orpah? Is God speaking to you, showing you similarities between your life and the life of Orpah?

I pray that the information written throughout this book will prompt you to examine your life. I encourage you to utilize the "Steps on the Journey" note section at the end of each chapter to reflect and look deep within yourself. Pray to God and ask Him to help you examine yourself. Write whatever He instructs you to write. Don't be afraid of the transformation process. This is only to help you "Change your name." I also pray that this book will lead you to a freeing, healing, forgiving of self, in the name of Jesus Christ our Lord.

It is my pleasure to have freely shared parts of my life with you in this book and I do it with love, knowing ministry is taking place. It's true all of us have a story to tell and it's only by the grace of God that we can tell our story. Satan has tried to keep me quiet. Many times while writing, a negative voice would say, "You do not want anyone to know your story, your issues, or the challenges your face in your life." The voice would continue by saying, "People will not listen to your message if they learn these things about you." Other times the voice would say, "The sisters are going to talk about you." But God would say, "I'm setting you free." Other times God would say, *"Your testimony is not for you, but for you to share with someone else."* I pray that my "freedom" likewise will set you free. Now that my story has been told, what can man do to me? Absolutely nothing! I'm no longer living in secrets. I'm no longer living in the dark, for I have allowed the Lord to shine His light on all of my dark places, and I lovingly open the door for you to be liberated to share your story. Now it's your turn to be set free from the secrets you have held so close and allow the Holy Spirit to move and expose those areas that have held you bound. Once you are free, please reach back and lead someone else to freedom. I am praying with and for you.

ARE YOU READY TO CHANGE YOUR NAME?

Pray with me.

Dear Lord, we ask that You would reign in each of us, for we are Your children. Open our ears and our hearts unto You. O God, we pray that You would deal with our flesh so that we would walk in the Spirit of God and not the spirit of self. Please deliver a fresh Word unto Your people. Father, we pray that You would transform each of us suddenly. Let us decrease that You may come forth in our lives with boldness and power. This we pray in the name of Jesus.

I pray that when this is all said and done that many will say, "What must I do to be saved?" and others will say, "What must I do to turn my life around?"

ONE

IS YOUR NAME ORPAH?

Orpah was the woman who was known by some to be the woman who rejected her chance. Some have said that Orpah means "double-minded," which can describe her position on the road to Bethlehem when her mother-in-law, Naomi, suggested that she and her sister-in-law, Ruth, return to their homeland, Moab. The book of James reminds us, "A double-minded man is unstable in all his ways." (James 1:8) As you read the book of Ruth you will find that Ruth continued on with Naomi; however, Orpah made the decision to return to Moab. The Bible says in Ruth 1:14, "At this they wept again. Then Orpah kissed her mother-in-law goodbye, but Ruth clung to her."

> "At this they wept again. Then Orpah kissed her mother-in-law good-bye."
>
> **Ruth 1:14**

Yes, that's right! Orpah turned from them and went her own way. Orpah made the choice to return to the rich and prosperous Moab she once knew. Moab was in her heart. After embracing Naomi, Orpah went home to be with her own people and to her own gods. With a kiss to Naomi, she separated from the only true and living God. After that kiss, Orpah vanished from the pages of Holy Scripture. After that kiss to her mother-in-law, you never hear of Orpah again. What a price to pay for turning back. Allow me to ask: Can you relate to any of the characteristics Orpah displayed? Could your name be Orpah?

Take a moment and think back over your life. What do you see? Do you recognize a pattern? Do you find yourself unsure, afraid, and needing to stay in the familiar? I can remember saying things like, "This is too hard," and "It's not worth it." Although it was apparent that the task at hand was something I knew God had anointed me to do, I had to step outside the familiar in order to move to the next level to experience what was ahead. Every day we are faced with life situations. One must realize and accept that this life we live is not going to be easy. It would be a no-brainer to dismiss our life journey and take the easy road; however, it is at this point of our journey we need to push through fear and insecurities, put our full trust in God, and allow Him to direct our path. If we are trusting in God we can move forward knowing He is with us regardless of our fears. When in doubt, we must ask ourselves, "Did God tell me to do this or was it an act of self?"

Imagine allowing God to fully orchestrate your life. The Bible says in Jeremiah 29:11, "For I know the plans I have for you," declares the Lord, "plans to prosper you and not to harm you, plans to give you hope and a future." God has already shared with you through His Word that He plans to give you prosperity and hope. Why then do we go about our business orchestrating our own life? "Trust in the Lord with all your heart and lean not on your own understanding; in all your ways acknowledge him, and he will make your paths straight. (Proverbs 3:5,6) If only we would trust God, life would be so much better. I didn't say that life would be easy, but it would definitely be better.

The Word of God says, "He who dwells in the shelter of the Most High will find rest in the shadow of the Almighty." (Psalm 91:1) To rest in the shadow of the Almighty means to let go. Don't worry. Do not wrestle against flesh and blood. Free yourself to think on things that are true, pure, lovely, and of a good report. To worship God is to rest in Him. When we rest in the Lord, there's sweet peace. When we rest in God we can breathe.

Orpah in her own way embraced Moloch, the heathen god of Moab. This was her personal way of worship. Her way of worship led her to never be mentioned again in the Holy Scriptures. It is easy to get caught up in our own gods, which may lead us to worshiping things instead of worshiping the only true and living God. Take a moment and ask, "What god am I worshiping?" Take it a step further and ask, "What do I need to cleanse from my life in order to fully worship the only true and living God?"

The Bible is our blueprint. In order to understand and live within the path the Lord has set before us one must refer to it often. It's sad to say, but the Bible becomes the last resort in seeking answers when it should be the first place we turn. Everything we need to know about our life plan can be found in the Word of the Lord. However, we have made the choice throughout our life to replace our study and meditation time with watching television, talking on the telephone, and surfing the Internet, engaged or enthralled in social networking. We face many distractions in this life. These distractions take us off course and could lead us to a plan that does not have our name on it. It is as if we are standing before several opportunities looking for something different than what God has already spoken. We are looking for easy when God is saying, "I know what's best — go this way."

God has a plan for you — Trust Him!

STEPS ON THE JOURNEY

Do you see a connection between your life and the life of Orpah?

_____

_____

_____

If your answer is yes, what is the connection?

_____

_____

_____

_____

Every one of us has issues. What issues do you believe that Orpah struggled with during her lifetime?

_____

_____

_____

_____

What are some of the issues you struggle with in your life?

_____

_____

_____

_____

_____

Can you relate to Orpah's dilemma? Explain.

_____

_____

_____

_____

_____

_____

_____

Is jealously a part of Orpah's actions? Why or why not?

_____

_____

_____

_____

_____

_____

_____

Have you been in a situation like Orpah's? Please explain your answer.

_____

_____

_____

_____

_____

_____

_____

If you answered "yes" in the previous question, were you pleased with your decision? Please explain.

_____

_____

_____

_____

_____

_____

_____

Are you ready to change your name? Why?

_____

_____

_____

_____

_____

_____

Let's Pray.

Father, in the name of Jesus, I'm ready to do as You would have me to do.

"YOUR FAITH HAS HEALED YOU..."
Matthew 9:22

"Those Sinful Twin Sisters"

"The acts of the sinful nature are obvious:...jealousy... envy..." (Galatians 5:19-21)

JEALOUSY is the fleshly disapproval for how God is blessing somebody else. Its twin sister ENVY is wanting for yourself what somebody else has. In either case, these selfish attitudes express a deep disregard and disrespect for God. You literally communicate to God, "I don't like how You are treating me." Sister girl...Get over it! Here is your prescription for healing from jealousy and envy:

1) Accept the fact that you don't control, dictate, or communicate to God what He is to do. The Lord knows exactly how to bless you. Maybe the reason He won't bless you like you want is because of your attitude.

2) Ask God's forgiveness and continued cleansing of your heart. (1 John 1:9)

3) Begin praising God for what you have *(and what you do not have)*. (1 Thessalonians 5:18)

Just as important is being able to praise God for how He chooses to bless others. (Romans 12:15) Swallow these three pills and look for God to work in your life.

Be healed in the name of Jesus from "jealously!"

TWO

DON'T TURN BACK!

One day several years ago, while living in Atlanta, Georgia, my husband came to me and said, "I need to share with you what God is doing in my life." I sat there while he explained to me that God had placed a call upon his life to minister the Gospel of Jesus Christ. He explained that we would have to leave Atlanta and move to Columbus, Ohio, where he was to pursue his Master in Divinity degree. I felt as though I was leaving a "good life." You know that so-called "rich and prosperous" life that Orpah was returning to as she once knew? I was leaving that behind. Atlanta is believed to be a city of status and prestige, a place where my husband's family lived and which I had grown to call home, a place that gave me a sense of security and where I began to grow wings and hoped to one day fly. That was the place God had directed us to leave and to go to a place of a new beginning.

Understand me: I was comfortable. I lived in a house that many only dream of owning. I enjoyed the large walk-in closets, three large bedrooms, two baths, and the comfort of enjoying my Jacuzzi. We had an open living and dining room that overlooked the deck which lead to the inground pool. I felt as though I was on top of the world as a young married woman, wife, and mother.

I had forgotten all about the promises of God. I decided to write my own plan. I began to delay the process of moving by taking my time to pack boxes and in many cases filling my day with other things that would not allow me to pack at all. Just like Orpah, I was "double-minded." I would tell some people that I was excited about moving. I would tell others that I didn't want to move. On one hand I was saying to God, "I'll do whatever You want me to do," but on the other hand I was showing God that I didn't really trust Him.

I knew that God was moving in my life, but I had to stop living in fear. I could see the open door, but I was unable to see the other side of the door. I was vacillating back and forth. I felt the presence of God. However, there was a "*but.*" I'm sure you know what I'm talking about. You're waiting for some miraculous event to take place right before your very eyes. And then you realize you are not the one in control. One breath you shout "Yes!" but with the next breath you whisper, "What's the end result?" You desire for God to reveal the complete picture. And yet He keeps you guessing. You know He will not mislead you, but you still would like to know more of the plan then He's communicating. You have this need for God to speak with the loud, audible voice and as He is speaking to you, the room you're sitting in shakes and someone blows a horn and behold, God is there. I know I'm not the only one who has had this thought. But that's not how God comes to all of His children. God was speaking. However, He was speaking to me through my husband. The message: It's time to move. I must leave what I have acquired behind. To some degree all I could hear was that it was time to start over. "Me, start over?" I asked. God replied, "Not start over, but move forward." There's a difference. Without a doubt, God was calling my husband and me to move forward. God was calling my husband and at the same time He was calling me. My challenge was that I didn't have a clear understanding of what exactly the Lord was calling me forward into. I had my plan but God had His plan and His plan had to interrupt my plan. His plan was designed to give me hope and a future. My plan could have led me to destruction, because remaining in a place He was moving me from would have delayed His plan for my life. Being disobedient could have resulted in misery, depression, oppression, heaviness, confusion, and being outside the will of the Lord.

"But Lot's wife looked back, and she became a pillar of salt."

Genesis 19:26

I continued to struggle with this move although I knew it was for the best. I came to realize that I had a serious flesh problem. You could say it was a tug-of-war. I could not quite understand the urgency of the move. At that time I had just given birth to a daughter, and thought there's no way I can move with a newborn. We had spent money on the nursery. It was a designer's original that communicated a "rich and prosperous city," per se. I recall sitting around the house asking myself, "What are you going to do? You don't have a job."

This move would include living in a seminary apartment. Going from 2,500 square feet to about 800 was not my idea of fun. What would my friends and family say about my decrease? I was living large and now I was downsizing, and not by choice. My mind was spinning out of control. "How will this look, living in a box apartment without sound insulation, hearing my neighbors three doors down?" "What will this do to my persona?" "What will my girls say?" "Will they want to hang out with me or will they talk bad about me?" On and on I had this voice in my head giving me every reason to look back and stay stuck on what was comfortable. "Turn back," the voice said. "Tell your husband to go on without you."

God began to minister to me. Genesis 19:26 says, "But Lot's wife looked back, and she became a pillar of salt." You know the story…

The two men said to Lot, "Do you have anyone else here — sons-in-law, sons or daughters, or anyone else in the city who belongs to you? Get them out of here, because we are going to destroy this place. The outcry to the Lord against its people is so great that he has sent us to destroy it." So Lot went out and spoke to his sons-in-law, who were pledged to marry his daughters. He said, "Hurry and get out of this place, because the Lord is about to destroy the city!" But his sons-in-law thought he was joking. With the coming of dawn, the angels urged Lot, saying, "Hurry! Take your wife and your two daughters who are here, or you will be swept away when the city is punished." When he hesitated, the men grasped his hand and the hands of his wife and of his two daughters and led them safely out of the city, for the Lord was merciful to them. As soon as they had brought them out, one of them said, "Flee for your lives! Don't look back, and don't stop anywhere in the plain! Flee to the mountains or you will be swept away!" But Lot said to them, "No, my lords, please! Your servant has found favor in your eyes, and you have shown great kindness to me in sparing my life. But I can't flee to the mountains; this disaster will overtake me, and I'll die. Look, here is a town near enough to run to, and it is small. Let me flee to it — it is very small, isn't it? Then my life will be spared." He said to him, "Very well, I will grant this request too: I will not overthrow the town you speak of. But flee there quickly, because I cannot do anything until you reach it." (That is why the town was called Zoar.) By the time Lot reached Zoar, the sun had risen over the land. Then the Lord rained down burning sulfur on Sodom and Gomorrah — from the Lord out of the heavens. Thus he overthrew those cities and the entire plain, including all those living in the cities — and also the vegetation in the land. But Lot's wife looked back, and she became a pillar of salt. (Genesis 19:12-26)

When I read the story in Genesis 19, I heard God saying, *"Don't look back; I have a plan for you."* Lot's wife looked back and because she looked back she became a pillar of salt. Orpah turned back and she vanished from the pages of Holy Scripture. If you turn back, how will this interrupt what God has planned for you? Don't let that be a setback for you. "Move forward; trust Me," God says.

"Never look at what you are leaving; look at what or where God is taking you."

Let's examine the word "turned." It means to change the direction or course, to divert or deflect, to change the purpose, intention or content, to change order or disposition. It also means to cause to go in a specific direction or to be direct. Orpah turned back. Turning back also means to switch one's loyalty from one side to another. Lot's wife looked back, which was a change in direction. She looked back to see what she was leaving. I strongly encourage you not to look back. God has greater things ahead for you. We must learn to trust Him.

God was telling me that with Him all things are possible. He was putting me through what I believed to be a test, just as I believe that Naomi was putting Orpah through a test. Our God is a gentle and kind God; He won't force you to do anything that you truly don't want to do. We have a choice. God gives us a choice.

Although my life would change as it relates to material possessions and being connected to the world, my life would change for the better. We benefit by taking the path God has set before us. There are many benefits to taking the path of God. God makes it very clear: "In order to receive all that I have for you, I need you to proceed **_My_** way."

The stress that my life endured during the resistance to moving created a brief setback in my Christian walk. I became "double-minded." My spirit was saying, "Yes, I will follow Jesus," and my flesh was saying, "I have an image to portray." Once I got myself together to follow only God, my life took yet another turn. It hit me. With the difference in the square footage we had to sell much of our furniture. This was earth shattering! I realized everything that I would have to give up in order to move forward. Depression and the spirit of oppression tried to creep in. However, we moved to Columbus into the seminary apartments. We were fortunate to have a three-bedroom apartment, but it had outside-texture carpet, walls that allowed you to hear exactly what your neighbors were saying, and windows that you rolled open with one crank. Follow me for a moment: You know the crank that you use to roll open a window? When I say that we had one crank, I'm saying that once you open one window, you remove that crank and open the other window. Get the picture? It took me a moment to get used to the living conditions.

With my husband being a full-time seminary student, I knew that I needed to find employment. Money was starting to run very low. God surrounded us with family and friends who would have showed their love and support; however, I had way too much pride to share with them the position we were in due to the sacrifice we made in order to move forward into what the Lord was leading us to. I never really wanted my parents to know that we were without food on many occasions, so I kept them in the dark concerning our living conditions as we struggled to make it through. I would simply show up around meal times at my parents' home and casually accept their invitation to stay and eat since I was already there. I pretended as if I was already preparing a meal, but I know my mom and dad well enough to know that they would insist that we stay and eat. Truth—that was manipulation. I found myself manipulating my parents. That could not be of God. I needed to humble myself and speak the truth. While I was out seeking employment the children were being fed at my parents' home. Nothing more I knew my children were eating healthy meals. Here's the truth; I was not pulling the wool over their eyes. They knew what was going on. They had to have known. I think back and would say that they went along with my foolishness so that I might keep what I believed to be my dignity. My friend Brenda Troy would pop up at my home with bags of food saying, "Girl, I was out and thought I would pick you up a few things."

I can remember when my son, who was around eight years old at the time, asked for some Rice Krispies™ treats. His dad went to the store and had enough money to buy the off-name brand. He came home, made the batch of treats, and tried to pass them off as the real thing to our son. They were absolutely awful. My husband had made a full pan but after one bite we threw the remaining treats in the trash. Although a relatively insignificant incident, it was just another reminder that I didn't like the sacrifices we were making.

I can remember asking God this question, "If You love us, and if we are in Your will, why is this happening to us?" I can still hear to this day God say, "Just trust Me." So I trusted Him. I began to avail myself to God and His plan with the move to Columbus, Ohio. I laid down my control and started to rest in Jesus. I thought "life was going just fine." God had already worked out the plan. Being that I was born and raised in Columbus, I had all of my siblings, parents, and grandparents there. I had lived there basically all of my life except for the few years in Atlanta. God opened the door to return to a previous place of employment with better pay and a promotion. My mother took care of my daughter. My son was in a well-known and highly recognized educational system. My husband was in seminary with all expenses paid. That led him to the open doors to study under the leadership and become a son in the ministry to Dr. Charles E. Booth, pastor of Mt. Olivet Baptist Church in Columbus, Ohio, and to Dr. Keith A. Troy, pastor of New Salem Missionary Baptist Church in Columbus, Ohio. Serving under great leadership led him to a greater ministry of Jesus Christ. By the way, the day my husband went to the store for the off-brand Rice Krispies™ treats, he met a gentleman who happened to be the Christian Education Director at Mount Olivet. They were looking for a Youth Minister and you guessed it, one thing led to another. What more could one ask for?

What about your life? Can you look back over your life and give thanks to God because you didn't turn away and go back to what may have represented less than what God wanted for you even when you had to face some difficulty and sacrifice? What would your life look like if you simply continued to do things to please others and lived in order to gratify your flesh?

Looking at Orpah; she did not know what could have been ahead. She made the choice to end her travel with Naomi and Ruth. She believed that she knew all there was to know about her homeland, Moab. Orpah turned back instead of moving forward. This life is about trusting God. He gives us a choice to follow Him or not. I made the choice to follow Him. I'll let you in on a little secret: I followed Him, but I cannot say that at that time I trusted

Him. Truth ~ I thought, "What do I have to lose?" *(just keeping it real)*

When we're traveling the road before us, it can often be difficult. The next turn in my life came just when things seemed to be returning to normal. Here comes God revealing more of His plan. You know how it is: just at the moment you get comfortable, settled, ready to take a breath, God says, "Now..." *(you fill in the blank)*

My husband and God had been talking. After God spoke with him, he came to me saying, "Babe, I have something to share with you. The Lord said that by my birthday I am going to pastor a church." I didn't say anything immediately, but inside I was screaming, *Yeah, right!* That was my thinking. *"Where?"* was my other question. My husband continued the conversation by telling me that Rev. Leon Troy Sr., the pastor that married us, told him of a church in Oberlin, Ohio, that had been without a pastor for quite some time. I can remember saying, *"Where is Oberlin?"* not realizing that God had already worked things out behind the scenes. Let me share with you how God works.

Through my work in Columbus, I met a woman who asked me to come to her agency to conduct a workshop at a conference she was hosting. I would travel back and forth to Cleveland on the main interstate. During a conversation, she shared with me a way to cut time on my travel. She recommended that I travel the back roads until I could exit onto the highway. Now, you know how the enemy comes in and tries to interrupt the plan of

God. Fear set in with me as it related to traveling the back roads. You know—an African-American woman traveling alone on the back roads at night. Get the picture? God immediately stepped in because He had a plan.

Once again let me remind you of what Jeremiah 29:11 says, *"I know the plans I have for you, declares the Lord, plans to prosper you, give you a hope, not to destroy you or cause destruction."* I was running late for a training session coming from Columbus and noticed the exit for the back roads: I prayed, then I exited. I realized that traveling the back roads saved me time and I enjoyed the beautiful, peaceful scenery. I even stopped several times on my return home in a little town that had wonderful art and music. It reminded me of Mayberry. While traveling to visit the church in Oberlin with my husband, to my surprise, he exited at the same exit I would take on my travel to Cleveland. He stopped in the town that I would often visit to shop. The town was Oberlin, the town that the church was located. See how the Lord works? This is called "preparation." He prepared me. He's preparing you. Don't turn back. Oh, by the way, as sure as my name is Gail, God called my husband to pastor right before his birthday. He was called to Mount Zion Baptist Church in Oberlin, Ohio, where he served as pastor for five years.

You see, I sincerely thought that I was losing everything that we had built in the six years while living in Columbus. I was entering a foreign land that I thought I knew nothing about. I pray that you are taking this in. I'm trying to help someone who may be going through a similar situation and in the midst of a struggle with flesh and Spirit. Don't turn back. Please, follow and trust God. It doesn't matter what people think, say, or do. Only God matters. He has a plan for you. Don't turn back. I'm sharing my story with you to prayerfully set you free from the bondage of being bound by others and fear of not knowing.

My testimony is not only for me. My testimony to the providence of God is to share with you as you also may have to travel a sometimes unpredictable journey. It's not easy. (Nobody promised you easy!) There are times when I think about turning back today. But I can't! God has been that good to me, and continues to shower me with His blessings. He doesn't give me everything I want; however, He opens up the windows of Heaven and pours out to me blessings upon blessings. God's hand of favor is and has always been upon me. Sometimes I wonder what my life would look like if I had turned back. Praise be to God that I didn't turn back. Now, I am encouraging you to stay on the path that God has designed for you. You may not be able to see it all or understand it all, but don't turn back! You may not have all the answers, but don't turn back! You may not be comfortable, but don't turn back!

Pray with me.

Father, in the name of Jesus, please give me Your strength not to turn back. I can't see my way, but I am trusting You. Thank You for Your promises. Thank You for giving me a hope and a future. Thank you for all that You do. Every time I think about turning back, I will look up. When I think about where I was compared to where I am and where You are taking me, I will hold on a little while longer.

**"Peace I leave with you; my peace I give you.
I do not give to you as the world gives. Do not let
your hearts be troubled and do not be afraid."**
John 14:27, NIV

STEPS ON THE JOURNEY

What have been some of the reasons you have wanted to turn back? Please explain.

_____

_____

_____

_____

_____

What does the Bible say about turning back, especially when God has instructed you to do something?

_____

_____

_____

_____

_____

Are you willing to ignore God to satisfy your flesh? Explain.

_____

_____

_____

_____

_____

Promise God that you won't turn back!

What is your testimony?

_____

_____

_____

_____

_____

_____

_____

_____

_____

_____

_____

_____

How many people have you shared your testimony
with? _____ Name them.

_____

_____

_____

_____

_____

_____

How many people has God placed in your life to share
your testimony with but for whatever reason you
haven't?

_____

If you have not shared your testimony with anyone, how do you feel about not sharing your testimony?

_____

_____

_____

_____

I'm praying and standing with you that you will share your testimony and set someone free in Jesus' name!

"YOUR FAITH HAS HEALED YOU..."
Matthew 9:22

"FAITH"

"But her delight is in the law of the LORD, and on his law she meditates day and night. She is like a tree planted by streams of water, which yields its fruit in season and whose leaf does not wither. Whatever she does prospers." (Psalm 1:2-3)

Many people find it reasonable to believe _in_ God. But do you _believe_ God? An active faith is belief, trust, surrender, dependence, obedience, and certainty in the Lord Jesus Christ. There are two other characteristics of an active faith that also must be considered: <u>CONFIDENCE</u> and <u>RISK</u>. To have an active faith is to delight in and mediate upon the Word of God and to be confident that what God says is true — so confident that she spends her life determined to hear what God is saying. By the power of the Holy Spirit, she will have the confidence to be planted like a tree and be able to stand through anything.

But don't stop there. When you have confidence, your faith will also move you to take a risk. After all, you believe God, don't you? Real faith moves you to bear fruit, refusing to let your leaf shrivel up. Step out there and dare to do the impossible for God. Dream your dreams, but do something about them. Hope for the best, but work to achieve the best. If God said it, have the courage to take the risk.

Confidence is your willingness to let the seed of Christ to be planted in your life. Risk is your availability to bring forth fruit by what you do for the Lord. God makes this promise: Whatever you do will prosper!

How much CONFIDENCE do you have?

_____

_____

_____

_____

_____

What is your dream?

_____

_____

_____

_____

_____

_____

What RISKS are you willing to take? List them below.

_____

_____

_____

_____

_____

THREE

REMOVAL OF THE MASKS

Real or phony? That is the question. Can we talk? I mean really talk? I would like for us to have the kind of conversation that is without the make-up, dress-up, use of proper words and such. It's just you and me letting our hair down and being real for a moment. Forget about who is watching or who we need to impress. Let's take off the mask and become upfront and personal and get to the real issues that we face in our lives about ourselves.

Allow yourself to move out of your comfort zone and think about the real you. Who are you? Take your time and get acquainted with you. I realize that this may be difficult so allow me to help you take the necessary steps to survive the big question: Who are you? Are you real or phony? No one has to know your answer but you. Be still for a moment and reflect on exactly who you are. Forget about your demanding boss, coworkers, friends, and family. Yes, everyone wants something from you and they want it right now! But do not worry yourself with them right now. I am asking you to think about *you* for a moment.

Ever found it difficult to get in tune with you? If so, close your eyes and dream of a more peaceful place— a place of crystal clear waters, beautiful sunrises, and breathtaking sunsets—a place where you can meet Jesus. A "safe place"; a place of letting go and allowing God to lead, guide, and direct you; a place in which you do not feel the pressure to do something outstanding, important, or fantastic for people to like, validate, or agree with. Enter into that safe place where you can be vulnerable and securely share with Jesus what you are experiencing. Tell Him your hurt, fears, and the areas where you may need inner healing. So often there are many of us who seek approval from others. After all, we reason, who could possibly like me for just being me? We repeatedly feel we need to do something more, so others will approve of us and love us. Everywhere we turn, we are faced with pleas for help. Our spouse, our boss, our children, our friends, our family, our elderly relatives all cry out for our time and attention, wanting us to do things their way, all based upon their approval. In your safe place with Jesus you will not have to experience any of those requests. Take time with Jesus and steal away into a resting place of peace and freedom.

Requests continue to stack up, demanding our attention. It is too difficult to say no, the guilt is too great. We fear that we may lose something or someone if we go against their request. So-called urgent demands are continually placed on our time and energy. Mask after mask we change to fit with the demand. The urgent becomes a tyrant, trying to make a slave of us to the point that we never accomplish those things that are important which line up with God and His purpose for our life. We are too busy trying to be someone else that we lose sight of who we are. What can we truly accomplish trying to live the life of someone else and not our own? And if that's not enough, we have such unrealistic expectations of ourselves that we become depressed and lost. Why are we so surprised at ourselves when we get sick or become tired, ready to give up and give in? Who are we trying to impress anyway? When do we take the time and ask God if this is His plan for us?

The Bible says in Philippians 4:8, "Finally, brother, whatever is true, whatever is noble, whatever is right, whatever is pure, whatever is lovely, whatever is admirable—if anything is excellent or praiseworthy, think about such things." When truth is revealed, we have the power to decisively and courageously take off the masks. Satan has lied to us long enough! It's not about what others have to say about you—it's what *God* has to say. God's Word is truth!

The first thing that I would like to suggest would be for you to face your flesh. This can be a very painful experience but a freeing experience as well. I can remember facing myself for the first time in my mid-thirties. I had to identify with who I was and who I had become in spite of what God had created me to be. I'm reminded that

God is a gentle and kind God; He won't force Himself on anyone. So He allowed me to be who I thought I wanted to be. I became negative and selfish, while spending my life trying to please others. This was not the life God had for me. But I was wearing so many masks that I didn't know which one was which. Yes, today I am free, I can talk about it now, and I want you to be free as well. I had to realize that the Creator wanted me to be who He created me to be. That meant that I had to remove all of the masks and walk in the shoes that were designed only for me. It took some pruning, cutting, and peeling to align my will with God's will. God taught me that no one needed to validate me but God Himself. What a freeing statement!

I had so many people trying to tell me who I was, what I needed, and who was the best one to do this and that for me. People would try to tell me what to wear and what I liked and didn't like. All along I knew what I wanted to wear, what I liked and disliked, and I knew what God was telling me; I just wasn't listening. I even had people telling me what was best for my husband. They would tell me what he wanted, liked, and disliked. I can remember when someone told me that I needed to minister to my husband, when I was already ministering to him. *Imagine that!* People actually became angry with me because I didn't agree with their thoughts and theories. When you go against people and take a stand for what you believe, and that belief differs from what others think you should do or say, people will begin to treat you in cruel and mean ways. I began to see sides of personalities that I didn't know existed. If you're not following God, you will get confused.

With all the masks I wore I lost sight of who God created me to be. I would wear one mask for my mother-in-law. I wanted her to like me. I wanted her to know that her son married the right women: me. I would wear a mask for my family. As I mentioned in the last chapter, I did not want them to know that the fridge was bare. I wore a mask for my husband so that he could focus on his studies and not on how I felt about not living as I had once lived. I wore masks to hide what was really going on. My friend would ask me if I needed anything and to see if all was well. Every time she would say, "Now G, if you need anything, just let me know." I would always respond with, "Girl, everything is just fine." A few of us had a saying that went like this, "If I'm lying, I will apologize." I had to apologize to her many times. It's one thing to be faithful and another to hide behind masks. As I wore those masks I realized that I was living a lie. I would change to please my mother-in-law, change to show that everything was alright with my parents, change to make my husband think that everything was okay, change to please the people around me. Living with these masks interfered with what God was doing with me. I had to remove the masks.

I'm encouraging you to remove your masks. Early in my adult life I allowed people to dictate how I lived. Unfortunately, I ended up following them and not God.

This was a costly mistake, a mistake that I plead with you not to make. Could it be that I may have been insecure? Maybe. Whatever it was, it made for an open door to let my fleshly desires take over; and it also opened the window for Satan to sneak in. As a matter of fact, he didn't sneak, he walked boldly right on in. These are traps that the enemy sets for us. Beware of the traps.

Recall Orpah's dilemma. Was it possible that she was confused, seeking comfort and security in what was familiar to her? I have come to the conclusion that Orpah was a sister who may have been insecure, full of fear, scared of the unknown, double-minded, possibly stuck in her ways, jealous, self-centered, and perhaps a people pleaser. When we get to this point, it's only by the grace of God that we don't lose our mind. When you are pleasing people and juggling masks you don't know who you are from one day to the next. Am I this person today or that person? And if we read between the lines, Orpah was wearing so many masks that on the day she was traveling, being double-minded as she was, "I'm going," "I'm turning back," she didn't know which mask to wear when. She was confused just as you and I get confused sometimes. When we reach a state of confusion, we have to know that God's grace is sufficient. When we come to a roadblock in life, as we all have, or will, and we're unsure which way to turn, be assured that the only way to turn is to God. He will direct our paths. He'll tell us what to do. The time is now that we need to remove our masks and follow God. Don't wait; do it now! Remove those masks!

Orpah vanished from the Holy Scriptures and was never heard of again. Did she miss her destiny? How do we get to a place where we obey the Spirit of the living God and get away from our flesh? We must learn to boldly and courageously face our flesh and not follow our flesh. I've heard preachers say, "What is gained in the flesh must be maintained in the flesh." The dead ends, routines, ruts, mind-sets, habits, the likes of being double-minded, the need to please people, the emotional roller coasters, the conflict with self and others, the torments and self-centeredness — these issues hold our flesh in bondage. These are masks that we create.

Please realize that our greatest enemy is the flesh! Orpah's enemy, your enemy, my enemy, is our flesh! The flesh will kill, steal, and destroy. It's the enemy. We so often want to place blame on Satan. No, we need to look at ourselves. What are we doing? Our flesh creates an overwhelming sense of our own importance or greatness. Our flesh is self-seeking, rude, and cynical; it desires to ascend to the top at any cost of others, wants to make a name for itself, and will step on others to achieve that goal. Our flesh resents correction or suggestions, resents constructive criticism, seeks praise for worldly possessions, desires praise from people, feels it's important to have a particular title, an inflated public persona, improperly uses large and complex words in order to inflate its own ego, is touchy and easily offended, brags, boasts, and believes it is better than others. Here's the truth of the matter: when operating in the flesh, we fail to see our own ignorance and don't know who we are or Whose we are. In the words of Joyce Meyer, "Refuse to live in your flesh!" Flesh resists God. We must give this baggage, all this stuff, to God.

Paul pleads with us in the book of Romans to give our bodies as a living and holy sacrifice. Therefore we have to understand that in order to be transformed in the manner that is truly acceptable to God, we have to break down the walls of our inner self that remain as unredeemed, unsurrendered, unenlightened areas of our flesh. In case you're still missing the point, allow me to bring it a little closer to home. Flesh Syndrome: "You have failed to meet my needs," "You have not met my expectations," "You have not satisfied me or my desires," "You are insensitive to me," "You don't care about me," "I have to think of my happiness," "I owe it to myself," "I deserve to do this for a little while," "I have my rights," "I do not have to put up with this," "I can't take it anymore," "I'm leaving." Have you said any of these things? Go back to Orpah for a moment while she was walking the road to Bethlehem with Naomi and Ruth. At one moment, she was wearing the mask of people pleasing and yet at another moment she wanted to do her own thing. She changed her masks back and forth. She wanted to do her own thing, yet also wanted to please Naomi.

Here's a question: Could Orpah have been in competition with Ruth? Ruth is standing with Naomi. She wanted to be with her people and make Naomi's God her God. Was Orpah waiting on Ruth to make the first move? Who or what are you waiting on? Who are we seeking our approval from? The Bible says in the book of Psalms that "We are wonderfully made." We are uniquely made by God. There is no one else like you but you. **Sister, take off your mask and reveal your true self!** Again, no one has to validate us but God. God wants our obedience. He desires that we be obedient to His will and His way. Has God called you to do something, but you're not sure which mask you have on?

Because of the images we feel that we must portray, we wear masks to cover up some of these actions, not realizing that the covers must soon fall whether we want them to or not. After a while it's hard to keep up with the daily masks one wears. Just think: We wear our work mask, church mask, friendship mask, all the many relationship masks, and underneath it all is our real self. Who are you?

Will the real

_____

(put your name in the blank)
please remove your mask and become the person that God has ordained for you to be?

Let me warn you in advance. Removing your masks my cause you to lose friends and may even cause people to talk badly about you. Showing who you really are may literally change your world. But you need to know that it's okay. I'm a living witness that living according to who God created you to be is the most freeing experience that you will ever know. I have had people say to me, "What's going on with you? You never used to act like this." My response is, "There's nothing going on with me. You just have never known the real me."

I have even reintroduced myself to people. "Hello, I'm Gail E. Dudley." "I'm God's child." "I now live to please Him." If this makes people uncomfortable and they walk away from you and whatever relationship you had with them, **THAT'S THEIR PROBLEM, THEIR ISSUE, NOT YOURS!**

Let's pray.

> *Father, in the name of Jesus, help me to remove the masks that are hiding me from being me. Please give me the strength to be who You have created me to be. Let me realize that no one has to validate me but You, Lord.*

STEPS ON THE JOURNEY

Think about the masks that you wear on a daily basis and describe how you feel about each mask.

_____

_____

_____

_____

_____

_____

_____

Do you ever forget which mask you are wearing? Explain.

_____

_____

_____

_____

_____

_____

How many masks are you wearing?_____ Why?

_____

_____

_____

_____

_____

_____

As God gives you the strength to remove each mask, how do you think your life will be different? Explain.

_____

_____

_____

_____

_____

_____

_____

Why do you hide behind the masks in your life?

_____

_____

_____

_____

_____

_____

_____

What relationships do you believe you'll lose if you remove your mask? Explain.

_____

_____

_____

_____

_____

_____

_____

What's your greatest fear in the removal of each mask?
Please describe in detail.

_____

_____

_____

_____

_____

_____

_____

_____

_____

_____

_____

_____

_____

Please Note:

**This process will not conclude overnight.
Be patient and know that God is God.**

"Your mask is hindering the real you."

"YOUR FAITH HAS HEALED YOU..."
Matthew 9:22

"Revive Us Again!"

"Search me, O God, and know my heart; test me and know my anxious thoughts. See if there is any offensive way in me, and lead me in the way everlasting." (Psalm 139:23,24)

Exercise: Please get one paper plate, crayons, or markers and do the following:

- Prepare the paper plate as if you were preparing for Sunday morning church service. (Think about all that you do before you attend church. i.e., clothes, make-up, shoes, hair, etc.)
- Dress the paper plate from head to toe. I am not talking about how you feel but how you want to look for other people. This is your plate so please be honest.
- Draw on your hair. If you wear a hat to church, draw a hat.
- Draw your make-up as you would for Sunday morning service.
- Draw your Sunday best. And yes, put on those pumps.
- Spray your plate with the perfume that you wear.

NOW...let's have a real revival!

When I think of Revival, words come to mind that say: redefine, restore, rejuvenate, rebirth, resuscitation, resurrection.

When I think of why one may need reviving I think of the word LIFELESS...and as I searched for meaning to this word, I found words like: dead, expired, gone, dull, and spiritless. When I think about being lifeless, without a life and dead and expired, I think of the Only One who can revive me, Jesus the Christ. As hard as it may be, you and I have to remove the masks, the layers of the false self that have consumed our lives to the point where we have become lifeless, dull, and spiritless.

A real revival is having an intimate relationship with God. A real revival is allowing God to deal with you in such a unique and refreshing way. A real revival is becoming transparent, allowing people to see you for who you really are. A real revival is allowing God to resuscitate the dull spirit that is within you. A real revival is awakening the gifts and talents that are sleeping inside of you. A real revival is allowing the One who created you to take total control of your life. A real revival is allowing God to take your fragmented self along with the pain and agony of your life and restore your soul to where you depend completely on Him. A real revival is chasing God like a deer pants for streams of water. A real revival is going to Jesus and taking a drink of His living water.

EXAMINE YOUR PAPER PLATE!

Do you like what you see? Is there anything that you are hiding? Are you trying to deceive yourself or others by wearing a disguise? Listen to me: that mask that you are wearing, the one where you are trying to hide your insecurity, low self-esteem, your true finances, your marriage issues, your loneliness, your pain, your brokenness, envy, jealousy, and sadness, is only prolonging what God is trying to do for your and through you. God is saying to you right now: It is time for this masquerade to be over! God is waiting to set you free! Allow God's resurrection power to destroy your masks!

If you are led and only when you are ready, tear up your paper plate but do not stop there; remove those false masks that are hiding the true you!

FOUR

TRANSFORMATION BEGINS

The Bible says in Romans 12:2, "Do not conform any longer to the pattern of this world, but be transformed by the renewing of your mind." The New Living Translation says it like this, "Don't copy the behavior and customs of this world, but let God transform you into a new person by changing the way you think."

"Don't copy the behavior and customs of this world, but let God transform you into a new person by changing the way you think."
Romans 12:2, NLT

Transformation is the act or the instance of transforming or the state of being transformed. This is a continuous action by the Holy Spirit, which goes on for a lifetime. It is our responsibility as Christians to stay open to the process. Followers of Christ are not to be conformed to the values or behaviors of this world. We are to continue in a renewal process of ridding ourselves of our flesh and walking continuously in the Spirit of Christ. The renewing of our mind is developing a spiritual perception by learning to look at life on the basis of God's view of reality. I've come to understand what Paul is saying. Our minds need to be changed and transformed. We must present our bodies as a living and holy sacrifice unto the Lord. Our minds have to be changed regarding how we view others, how we view ourselves, how we view God, and how we view life situations. The Bible says in 2 Corinthians 3:18, "And we, who with unveiled faces all reflect the Lord's glory, are being transformed into his likeness with ever-increasing glory, which comes from the Lord, who is the Spirit."

In Philippians 3:21 the writing of Paul puts it this way, "Who, by the power that enables him to bring everything under his control, will transform our lowly bodies so that they will be like his glorious body." Ephesians 4 starting with the twenty-second verse which says, "Throw off your old evil nature and your former way of life, which is rotten through and through, full of lust and deception. Instead, there must be a spiritual renewal of your thoughts and attitudes. You must display a new nature because you are a new person, created in God's likeness — righteous, holy, and true." (Ephesians 4:22-24, NLT)

To start the process, we must first offer ourselves as living sacrifices, holy and pleasing to God for this is our spiritual act of worship. (Romans 12:1) To give your-self as a living sacrifice means to give yourself to God by how you live. We are to worship God in spirit and in truth. Please give me a moment to explain worship. In 2 Chronicles 7:14 the Bibles says that "If my people, who are called by my name, will humble themselves and pray and seek my face and turn from their wicked ways, then will I hear from heaven and will forgive their sin and will heal their land." The word "humble" in Hebrew is actu-ally *Kana`*, which means "to worship." We must humble ourselves before God.

What is worship? Worship is the ability to look to God and bow yourself humbly before Him and His will even in the face of what may seem to be a horrible life situa-tion. We must realize that our life is dependent upon our worshiping God in spirit and in truth. Our worship may take place in our office as we think about the blessing of having a job, in our home while we're cleaning, cooking, or doing laundry. Worship may also take place as we stare in our closets viewing our clothing choice. Worship may also take place in our bathroom as we shower, and yes, while on the commode. I for one have spent plenty of time worshiping God in a confined space reading my Bible. God has answered many prayers during that time, and I have gained revelation knowledge while in the bathroom. It's amazing how we may wake at two in the morning thinking we have to use the bathroom when in fact it is God drawing us closer to Him, and wanting to share His Word. I have met Jesus many times in the bathroom. Worship may take place in the car or while shopping. Worship does not just happen in the church building, but everywhere you go. Worship is a lifestyle. Let your worship be your sacrifice. Once you have accomplished Step One you are well on your way in the transformation process.

"Worship is a lifestyle!"

Let's walk through Psalm 51:1-15.

"Have mercy on me, O God, according to your unfailing love; according to your great compassion blot out my transgressions. Wash away all my iniquity and cleanse me from my sin. For I know my transgressions, and my sin is always before me. Against you, you only, have I sinned and done what is evil in your sight, so that you are proved right when you speak and justified when you judge. Surely I was sinful at birth, sinful from the time my mother conceived me. Surely you desire truth in the inner parts; you teach me wisdom in the inmost place. Cleanse me with hyssop, and I will be clean; wash me, and I will be whiter than snow. Let me hear joy and gladness; let the bones you have crushed rejoice. Hide your face from my sins and blot out all my iniquity. Create in me a pure heart, O God, and renew a steadfast spirit within me. Do not cast me from your presence or

take your Holy Spirit from me. Restore to me the joy of your salvation and grant me a willing spirit, to sustain me. Then I will teach transgressors your way, and sinners will turn back to you. Save me from bloodguilt, O God, the God who saves me, and my tongue will sing of your righteousness. O Lord, open my lips, and my mouth will declare your praise."

After we have offered ourselves as a living sacrifice, holy and pleasing to God, we can move to the next step of the transformation process. That next step, Step Two of the process, is found in verse one of Psalm 51, which reads, "Have mercy on me, O God, according to your unfailing love; blot out my transgressions." God says in Isaiah 43 verse 4 that we are precious and honored in His sight. He also says that He loves us. God has blotted out our transgressions. Please remember — there is no condemnation for those who are in Christ Jesus. On top of that, God promises us that nothing will be able to separate us from the love of God that is in Christ Jesus our Lord. (Romans 8:1,39) Begin to confess your sins to God. Ask for forgiveness. What I find freeing is saying to God how sorry I am for whatever it is that I've done. He forgives me every time. Go ahead, ask God to have mercy on you and to blot out, erase, all of your transgressions. Realize that God is doing a work in you even now.

Let me suggest that you take time going through each step of this process. Don't rush. Reflect, pray, wait on God, and listen to what He is saying to you. Journal your answers on the pages in the back of this book. So often we want to rush through something to say that we've completed this or that, but what I am suggesting is that you take your time and walk in the light that God has ordained. This is about you and your relationship with God. You are worth the time spent completing this process. You'll be glad you took this time. Get yourself a cup of Soy No Water Chai and find a cozy spot in your home where you and God can spend some time together.

Step Three, we need to ask God to *"Wash away all of our iniquity and cleanse us from our sin."* (Psalm 51:2) When I pray this Scripture, over myself, I ask God to extract every possible impurity that may live in me, consciously or unconsciously. I ask Him to go to all the secret places in me and scrub me down, to get into every corner that is hard to reach and use whatever is necessary so that I may be cleansed. I think about cleaning my home. I can remember the time that my hands became raw due to the cleaning solutions I was using to clean my home. I was in the bathroom one morning and looked up and saw filth. It bothered me so that I began to work on that filth and ended up cleaning all day. If you would have walked into my house the smell of cleaning supplies would have slapped you in your face. My hands started to become raw and started peeling after being exposed to potent cleansers all day. I had developed flaky, peeling hands for several days and I was embarrassed to have my hands in that condition. Of course, someone did notice my hands and asked me if I had a skin condition. The flaking and peeling finally came to an end and my hands looked brand new! *(I just said something.)* When you allow God to cleanse you, the old stuff will begin to be transformed. This process will be uncomfortable, but when God gets through with you, you will be just like new.

In Step Four, we need to identify our transgressions and recognize our sin. (Psalm 51:3) List the areas in your life where you realize that you are repeating the same sin and examine why. Ask yourself, "Why am I repeating those things?" This may seem simple but it's not. Please take your time on this step and ask God to reveal what you need to know. We want to place blame on others but we really need to look at ourselves. You may not understand why I'm asking you to identify the sin in your life but once you complete this step you'll see things in a different light. Sometimes we are sinning and we don't realize it or see it as sin. I encourage you to examine and admit your own involvement in sin.

During Step Four we must understand that it's only against God and Him alone that we have sinned and done what is evil in His sight. (Psalm 51:4) Do you really want to disappoint God? I don't, but I realize that I do. When I do things because of what others may have done to me or when I follow my flesh instead of following the voice of the Lord, I am sinning against God and God alone. In the long run I have found that I'm disappointed because what I've done doesn't line up with the Word of the Lord. When someone has wronged you in any way and you want to seek revenge, stop, think, and know that vengeance is the Lord's. We are to "be kind and compassionate to one another, forgiving each other, just as in Christ God forgave you." (Ephesians 4:32) The next time you want to respond based on what your flesh is telling you, think about what reflection this will have on God.

In Step Five, it is important to recognize and accept that we were sinful at birth; sinful from the time that we were conceived. (Psalm 51:5) This knowledge doesn't give us the license to keep on sinning. Many people use Romans 7 as an excuse to sin. I would agree, that the very thing I say I am not going to do, that very thing I do, sometimes worst than I did before. Remember: there is only One who is perfect and it's our calling to become Christlike. So we are to strive to be the best Christian we can be.

You're now ready for Step Six, which is to be honest with God with our inner parts, because God teaches us wisdom in the inmost place. (Psalm 51:6) Exercise wisdom. Go to the Word of God and pray for wisdom over and over in your life. Take your time before you speak. Listen, pay attention. Get the focus off of yourself and put your focus on God and the wisdom that He teaches.

Step Seven begins the final cleansing process. Allow the Lord to use the strongest method necessary for this complete cleansing. Allow God to wash you. This kind of cleansing will make us whiter than snow. (Psalm 51:7) This goes hand in hand with the third step, except this time you mean it. You have gone through the other steps and now are taking this process more seriously. You have matured. You realize this is a process, and you have decided to continue to the end to see the powerful results of Jesus in your life. It is at this point that we have gained a better understanding and are ready to handle the cleansing process with confidence. You know what it's like when you move into a new place and you've cleaned in order to move your boxes and furniture into the new residence. But once you have set up your dwelling you look around and decide that you have to clean more thoroughly. This is Step Seven, asking and allowing God to cleanse you thoroughly.

Step Eight brings a sincere feeling of joy and gladness. After the Lord has crushed our bones, then we can rejoice. (Psalm 51:8) Have you ever had an ear infection? If so, you will understand this example that I will use to describe joy and gladness. I can remember when my ear ached so badly that I thought I had lost my hearing. I went to the doctor and he administered medicine in my inner ear that caused a loud pop! Immediately, I could hear and the aching stopped. I was pain free. What joy and gladness I felt after being able to hear and the pain stopped! Yes, it was painful and the pop raised me up off the table, but immediately — and I mean immediately — there was joy! This is how it is with God. He will break you, He will crush you, He will take away all that stuff that has you messed up inside, but when He is finished, praise be to God, you will rejoice, have unspeakable joy and overflowing with gladness.

Step Nine, we are asking God to hide His face from our sins and blot out all our iniquity. Notice that you repeat Step Two. You're asking God to get all of it. (Psalm 51:9)

Finally we ask God to "create in us a pure heart, and renew a steadfast spirit within us." And to seal the process we pray that God will not cast us from His presence or take His Holy Spirit from us. At this point we pray that God will restore to us the joy of His salvation and grant us a willing spirit to sustain us. (Psalm 51:10-12) We must have a pure heart. In Jeremiah 29:13 God states that we are to seek Him with all our heart. However, many of us have divided hearts. Things such as anger, lust, idols, bitterness, unforgiveness, and pride cripple and cloud our hearts. We have to ask God to give us a pure heart. It's imperative that we ask God not to leave us! Please God, do not cast me from Your presence. Pray and ask God never to leave you. I'll let you in on something, *He won't*! The Bible says, "Nothing can separate you from the love of God." I know for myself that God will never leave us or forsake us because that is what He promised. Pray that the Holy Spirit will take up residence in your entire being. God will restore you. He will revive you. It's that simple; ask. He will answer.

What does transformation mean? It means: conversion, a change of heart, a different attitude, motivation, and perspective. Transformation means, commitment; a change of way: faith that produces good character and action. And it means, confidence; change of life: radical dependence on the Lord and His Word. Romans

6:13 says, *"...give yourselves completely to God since you have been given new life. Use your whole body as a tool to do what is for the glory of God."* (NLT) Your transformation is well under way. You are starting to experience a taste of **FREEDOM**! Freedom is the state of your mind, heart, and soul and complete **PEACE** and in alignment with the will of God. The chains of bondage to the flesh have been broken. **Hallelujah!**

Transformation Complete

Step Ten – Psalm 51:10-12

Step Nine – Psalm 51:9

Step Eight – Psalm 51:8

Step Seven – Psalm 51:7

Step Six – Psalm 51:6

Step Five – Psalm 51:5

Step Four – Psalm 51:3,4

Step Three – Psalm 51:2

Step Two – Psalm 51:1

Step One – Romans 12:1

STEPS ON THE JOURNEY

Which process do you feel will be most difficult for you?
Please explain your answer.

_____

_____

_____

_____

_____

_____

What are some of the risks involved when you choose to
open our heart?

_____

_____

_____

_____

_____

Describe a time when you allowed yourself to face some
of your personal issues. What were the benefits?

_____

_____

_____

_____

_____

_____

**"It is for freedom that Christ has set us free.
Stand firm, then, and do not let yourselves be
burdened again by a yoke of slavery."**
Galatians 5:1, NIV

What is the major hindrance to experiencing God's transformation process?

_____

_____

_____

_____

_____

Name three ways people may react to your transformation.

1._____

2._____

3._____

How will your handle their reactions? Explain.

_____

_____

_____

_____

_____

Let's pray.

God, I love You and I need You. Here I am; cleanse me so that I may be whiter than snow. I surrender myself unto You.

"YOUR FAITH HAS HEALED YOU..."
Matthew 9:22

"Expect A Miracle!"

"She never left the temple, serving night and day with fasting and prayers." (Luke 2:37, NASB)

For years she waited. In the depths of her heart, she knew that something wonderful would happen if she remained faithful. Her desire to be ready for God outlived her youth and her marriage. Anna was no dummy and she was no slouch. She understood the way God moves is through the availability of people who diligently seek Him. Then one special day it happened. The Savior of the world appeared in the place she had so faithfully served. The beauty of this Gospel narrative is that the blessing and the miracle was that the Lord showed up in her ordinary life, and because of His presence, she was blessed. Anna's response was correct. She began giving thanks to God and continued testifying about His miracle-working power. What do you expect from the Lord? Start with the expectation of His presence and continue praising Him for all that He is going to do in your life and you will find that you are truly blessed.

Be available to God. Let the transformation begin!

FIVE

FROM DARKNESS INTO THE LIGHT

First John 1:5 reads; "This is the message we have heard from him and declare to you: God is light; in him there is no darkness at all." The Holy Scriptures continue by saying in verses six and seven, "If we claim to have fellowship with him yet walk in the darkness, we lie and do not live by the truth. But if we walk in the light, as he is in the light, we have fellowship with one another, and the blood of Jesus, his Son, purifies us from all sin." Don't waste your life by living a lie. We cannot claim to have fellowship with Christ and live our life in the dark. It's one way or the other. Every secret you tell creates darkness. Every area of your life that you keep secret is darkness, and becomes bondage. Think for a moment. Every time someone tells you something and they say, "You have to keep this to yourself," is this darkness? There's a difference between a secret and having a conversation in confidence. Hear me when I say that a secret can put you in a form of bondage that could harm you. Some secrets may cause you stress — and you know that stress can kill you.

Darkness is to lack or having very little light: lacking brightness: a dark day. Darkness is also characterized by gloom; It is dismal, threatening. The one definition I think best describes darkness is: concealed or secret; mysterious.

The Bible says, *"Then you will know the truth, and the truth will set you free,"* (John 8:32) and *"Finally, brothers, whatever is true…think about such things."* (Philippians 4:8) I'm not sure about you, but I'm tired of wasting so much precious time, gifts, and talents on things that are not of God, living in the darkness. I'm tired of spending time on things that are not true, things that are not pure, not right, not noble or not lovely. The truth is in the Word of God. The truth is God's light. This truth will set you free. As a friend of mine once said, "The truth will make you free." Look at it this way: truth equals freedom. Live in truth, you're free. Speak truth, you're free. Walk in the truth, freedom. Seek truth, freedom. Read the truth!

I'm tired of the bondage of lies, living in darkness, and the hidden truth. We get so caught up in living in darkness that we end up in a web of hearsay, false information, and assumptions, instead of truth. Start something new. Every time someone comes to you with information, ask them: "Is this the truth?" "Will this make me live in God's light or keep me in the darkness?" The next time you want to get out of something, don't lie. Tell the truth. When Satan whispers a lie, rebuke it and tell yourself the truth, God's truth. "And you will know the truth and the truth will set you free." Consider the words of Ephesians 4:17-18, "*Live no longer as the ungodly do, for they are hopelessly confused. Their closed minds are full of darkness; they are far away from the life of God because they have shut their minds...*". (NLT)

When you live in darkness you are allowing Satan to have a hold on you. The truth gets lost in the darkness. This allows for confusion. This brings about fear and fear is an illusion. It's something that appears to be real, but in actuality it's false. It has become a trick of your mind. You think something is so, but it is not so at all. It's made up. May I encourage you to remain in God's light?

Follow me a moment. Imagine that you're entering your home late in the evening. It is dark and cold outside. As you enter your home, you realize that your lights won't come on. As you feel your way through the darkness, you stumble and fall a few times. This is exactly what happens when you live your life in darkness, separated from God. You stumble, unnecessarily, far too often. It's not worth it! Paul urges us to "*Live a life worthy of the calling we have received.*" (Ephesians 4:1) People who live in darkness very often unsuccessfully seek help from non-Christians, secular self-help books, and worldly recovery programs. They may experience sleep deprivation, anxiety, and overwhelming guilt.

In the darkness Satan can keep his hands on us. He preys on our weaknesses while in the dark. Let it be known that Jesus alone has the power to bind the brokenhearted, set the captives free, and release people from the prison of emotional, psychological, and spiritual darkness. And just knowing about the Lord is not enough when the shackles of life have you bound and overwhelmed in darkness. When we intimately experience and become consumed with our Lord and Savior Jesus the Christ to find permanent freedom from this darkness, the shadows have no power in our lives.

"As a prisoner for the Lord, then, I urge you to live a life worthy of the calling you have received."

Ephesians 4:1

Although we may have to suffer some pain, God will use that pain to draw us to true faith and trust in His sufficiency. God desires us to embrace Him so that we will know the truth. My husband teaches a simple but profound principle: "Truth is what it is — truth!" Experiencing God, as you enter into the light and the truth of Jesus Christ, demands a painful but necessary season of shedding of darkness. God can transform darkness to bring us into His light, and in the process, transform our lives as well. As you go through the transformation process that was introduced in chapter four, you will find that transformation includes seasons of darkness that will effectively serve to purge your life of sin and self-centeredness. Review verses three, four, and seven in Psalm 51: God brings us from the darkness of our lives into His light by cleansing us of our sinful, self-centered ways. God does this so that the Holy Spirit can freely flow within the very fabric of our being.

STEPS ON THE JOURNEY

What does it mean to live your life in the light of God?

_____

_____

_____

_____

_____

_____

_____

How much time have you wasted on stuff that is not of God? Explain.

_____

_____

_____

_____

_____

_____

_____

List the sins that have the greatest hold on you. What are you going to do to free yourself from this bondage?

_____

_____

_____

_____

_____

_____

1 John 1:8 says, "If we claim to be without sin, we deceive ourselves and the truth is not in us." What are your thoughts on this Scripture?

_____

_____

_____

_____

_____

_____

_____

What do you feel you need to do so that you can walk in the light of the Lord?

_____

_____

_____

_____

_____

_____

_____

"Your Faith Has Healed You..."
Matthew 9:22

"Peace!"

"Peace Jesus leaves with you, His peace He gives to you. He does not give to you as the world gives." (John 14:27)

John 14:27 states, "Peace I leave with you; My peace I give you. I do not give to you as the world gives. Do not let your hearts be troubled and do not be afraid." (NIV)

How tragic it is that we labor through this life, settling for that which does not and can never satisfy us completely. Sure, we may find some measure of temporary satisfaction in extra hours in the workplace, mindless entertainment, material attainment, and conquests of worldly glory — but for what? For more trouble and more fear! Jesus declares to His disciples the promise of His peace literally guarantees fulfillment, completion, satisfaction, and meaning — qualities of authentic Kingdom living that mirror in this lifetime our eternal destination in glory. Don't settle for less. Discover and recover the awesome privilege of the abiding peace of the Lord Jesus Christ as you learn to trust Him more deeply, love Him more honestly, and surrender to Him more completely.

Move out of the darkness into His beautiful light!

SIX

HEALING IN HIS WINGS

"*Your faith has healed you.*" (Matthew 9:22) "Take up your mat and go…" (Mark 2:11) I began this book by sharing Orpah's journey with her mother-in-law and sister-in-law. I shared with you personal struggles and confusion I experienced early in adulthood. There were times that I could not see the light. I was afraid to face certain realities. I allowed situations to happen because I feared not pleasing people. I had fear and it was an illusion. I neglected the importance of pleasing God at the time.

When you allow God to come into your life and take charge, and you decide to follow Him, noticeable changes take place: good things happen. My life has changed in such a way that I know that I am a new creature in Christ. I feel brand new. Life is different for me now because I have realized what a difference living in obedience and the freeness of the Lord make. Yes, there will be difficult times ahead and tough decisions that have to be made; however, trusting in God will give you a peace that is indescribable.

We have a choice to make. God has given us free will. We have to make the decision to follow God or people. We can live our life for Jesus or people. We can strive to please God or people. I don't know about you, but I have decided to follow Jesus. THERE IS HEALING IN HIS WINGS! God kept me when I was down. Psalm 91 taught me how to "dwell in the shelter of the Most High." I experienced great pain when I was trying to please people. I realized that I could never truly please people. When you say "yes" to people, there will always be another demand or another request. Eventually, there will be a request or demand that you can't fulfill. I simply woke up one day and said, "Yes, Lord." The moment I said yes to God, I experienced many of my "so-called" friends leave my side. But God...He will never leave you nor forsake you. When God asks you to do something, He always equips you with everything you need.

In the midst of every pain, time of suffering, or personal challenge, God will show up with His power to set us free. However, we must invite Him in and allow Him to do all that He must do so that we can experience true deliverance in Jesus' name. The Bible says in Luke 13:12-13, "Woman, you are loosed from your infirmity...".

Consider the woman in Luke 13. She was the woman in the Bible who walked bent over with her face toward the ground for eighteen long years. She was unable to straighten up. Yet she was faithful to God. She attended synagogue Sabbath after Sabbath. She was so faithful that she ran into Jesus Himself. Jesus said, "Woman, you are healed!" Lift up your head! It's by no mistake that you are reading this book. I do believe that your season of deliverance is coming sooner than you think. You're probably saying to yourself, "This sounds good, but I have tried everything. I have prayed, fasted, I go to church, give seed offerings, had hands laid on me, and I have even lost sleep. Why hasn't my deliverance come?" Maybe your deliverance has not come because you are looking at your situation on a superficial level.

There's always a spiritual root to every emotional, physical, and psychological problem. It's deeper than that. We need to empty ourselves to discover fulfillment. I would suggest that you remain steadfast and unmovable in your desire to receive God's healing power. I understand that you may be walking around with a situation that is difficult for you to bear. Although crippled with this situation, find a Bible-based teaching church and study the Word of God to show yourself approved. Just like this woman in Luke; although crippled with a spirit, she found her way to the synagogue time after time. She was hungry for the Word of God. She faithfully made her way. So faithful she ran into the Lord Himself. Now it is your turn. Run straight for Jesus Himself!

"Trusting God will give you an indescribable peace."

When Jesus saw the woman, He called her forward and said to her, *"Woman, you are set free from your infirmity."* Then He put His hands on her, and immediately she straightened up and praised God." When I read this passage of Scripture I focus on the word "forward." "Forward" calls for us to have to push, move into, step into something with boldness and intentional action. We have access to the promises of God and His healing touch — if we just move forward. It is absolutely important that we refuse to get stuck in our circumstances and determine never to be consumed with our mess to the point that we can't appreciate what God is doing. The awful bondage of emotional sickness, physical sickness, psychological sickness, and even biological sickness keeps us in a prison of darkness if we allow ourselves to miss the Lord's grace at work.

God desires to liberate us. In fact, He has already done everything necessary to bring us liberation from anything that seeks to hold us captive. It is time that we understand what was accomplished on the cross. God's victory over sin and Satan makes our release from bondage of *"self"* possible. It's time that we face our stuff, believe God's Word, and refuse to remain in captivity sustained by Satan's accusations and attacks against us.

Believing in God's Word is our victory over insecurity, fear, wearing of masks, people pleasing, satisfaction with the darkness, or whatever else the captivity may be.

The good news is that the Lord Jesus came to set every captive free! How dare we stay in jail when we are free! You and I have been set free from sin and death; how dare we hold on to our chains! God has set you free! It's time to stand straight and strong in the freedom God has provided. Thank God for His awesome power. Thank God for His goodness. Thank God for His healing touch. Thank God for His deliverance.

"He who dwells in the shelter of the Most High will rest in the shadow of the Almighty."
Psalm 91:1

I'm not sure what was going on with Orpah or why she made the decision that she did. Orpah had a choice to make. She made the decision to "kiss her mother-in-law good-bye." Orpah then vanished from the pages of life. Did she do the right thing? Maybe the more relevant question is, *"Are you doing the right thing?"* Trust God and live!

"He who dwells in the shelter of the Most High will rest in the shadow of the Almighty. I will say of the Lord, "He is my refuge and my fortress, my God, in whom I trust."

Surely he will save you from the fowler's snare and from the deadly pestilence. He will cover you with his feathers, and under his wings you will find refuge; his faithfulness will be your shield and rampart. You will not fear the terror of night, nor the arrow that flies by day, nor the pestilence that stalks in the darkness, nor the plague that destroys at midday. A thousand may fall at your side, ten thousand at your right hand, but it will not come near you. You will only observe with your eyes and see the punishment of the wicked. If you make the Most High your dwelling even the Lord, who is my refuge then no harm will befall you, no disaster will come near your tent. For he will command his angels concerning you to guard you in all your ways; they will lift you up in their hands, so that you will not strike your foot against a stone. You will tread upon the lion and the cobra; you will trample the great lion and the serpent. "Because he loves me," says the Lord, "I will rescue him; I will protect him, for he acknowledges my name. He will call upon me, and I will answer him; I will be with him in trouble, I will deliver him and honor him. With long life will I satisfy him and show him my salvation." (Psalm 91:1-16)

Be encouraged ...

You are healed
In the name of
JESUS!

I Desire to Pray for You...

Most Holy and Awesome God, how excellent is Your Name in all the earth. The God of love who sits high and looks down below sending blessings and promises to Your people. I pray in the name of Jesus for the person who is holding this book right now. God, only You know exactly what they stand in need of. I lift up to You their very concern, their dreams and desires. In the name of Jesus I pray, "No weapons formed against them shall prosper." God, breathe into Your child new life. Open up the windows of heaven and pour them out a blessing that they will not have room enough to receive.

Ephesians 3:14-19 reads, "For this reason I kneel before the Father, from whom his whole family in heaven and on earth derives its name. I pray that out of his glorious riches he may strengthen you with power through his Spirit in your inner being, so that Christ may dwell in your hearts through faith. And I pray that you, being rooted and established in love, may have power, together with all the saints, to grasp how wide and long and high and deep is the love of Christ, and to know this love that surpasses knowledge that you may be filled to the measure of all the fullness of God."

I speak blessings, love, the power of God, life, anointing, encouragement, and opportunities into your life. I pray the blood of Jesus upon your life. I pray that you are blessed in an unusual way. I pray that your life will never be the same. I pray that one day soon I will hold in my hands a book that your will write and publish. I pray that the many gifts that God has placed on the inside of you will take you to the next level of Kingdom ministry. In the name of Jesus, AMEN!

STEPS ON THE JOURNEY

Are you ready to receive your healing? If not, what is standing in your way?

_____

_____

_____

_____

_____

_____

_____

Do you have enough faith to be healed? Explain.

_____

_____

_____

_____

_____

_____

Do you allow yourself to rest in the presence of the Lord? Why or why not?

_____

_____

_____

_____

_____

Do you understand that you have been set free by God sending His only Son to die for you and me so that we may be saved? On the third day He arose with all power in His hands! How does this make you feel?

_____

_____

_____

_____

_____

_____

_____

_____

_____

_____

What insight, if any, have you gained with regard to your life struggles, your past circumstances, and your present actions?

_____

_____

_____

_____

_____

_____

_____

_____

_____

_____

Ask God to heal you through writing your own prayer of healing below.

My Prayer

_____

_____

_____

_____

_____

_____

_____

_____

_____

_____

_____

_____

_____

_____

_____

_____

_____

_____

_____

_____

_____

_____

_____

"YOUR FAITH HAS HEALED YOU..."
Matthew 9:22

"Bless God!"

"I will bless the Lord at all times, His praise shall continually be in my mouth!" (Psalm 34:1)

The Bible says in Psalm 34:1 that we should bless the Lord at all times. The problem is that we are so preoccupied with everything and everyone that we don't take the time to bless God. With everything going on around us, our mind is not on praising Him. But...unless we bless God our circumstances will control our life. Blessing God is where our healing is!

I'm sure you are asking the question, "How do I bless the Lord?" I'm glad you have inquired. We bless the Lord with a willing spirit: a determined attitude. That means when you are down, bless God. When you are feeling depressed, bless God. When you do this, you feel better and your healing is taking place. You are not looking at your situation the same once you put your mind on Jesus and begin to bless Him.

Next, we bless God continually, which means ongoing, never ending, not to be interrupted. Therefore we should bless God daily, always, all the time. By continually praising Him we'll be—Declaring His Goodness. He is El Elyon the Most High God; He is Yahweh the Lord; He is Jehovah-Jireh, the Lord our provider; He is Jehovah-Shalom, the Lord or peace; He is Jehovah-Rapha, the Lord who heals; He is Awesome, He is Wonderful, He is Marvelous. He is who He says He is. And if you would only believe in Him and bless His name, your life will never be the same. You will know without a doubt that there is "Healing in His Wings!"

Make a list of why you want to bless the Lord:

_____

_____

_____

_____

_____

_____

_____

_____

_____

_____

_____

_____

_____

_____

_____

_____

_____

_____

_____

_____

SEVEN

TESTIFY
(READERS' TESTIMONIES)

First of all I would like to say thank you for taking the time to write your book, *Ready to Change My Name*. Your book has been an inspiration to my life as well as a blessing. One of the topics in your book that caught my attention was when you spoke on "wearing masks." I'm guilty of it. I have found it so easy to put on a front (mask) around people that rub me the wrong way. For example, I may put on a fake smile (knowing that it is not how I'm feeling) or I may avoid interacting with them at all. After reading your book I felt guilty (convicted) for not acting in a Christian manner. After all, who knows, that person or I could have been a blessing to one another. After reading your book it also made me look more within myself and wonder how could Lynette change her name and remove her masks. Well, by God's grace and the beautiful words in your book my transformation has begun.

Lynette L. Earl - LPN, OH

I believe that *Ready to Change My Name* will open the door for many to share their stories. Thank you for your honesty and transparency as you candidly shared some of your struggles and triumphs. I was inspired and encouraged by your sincerity, passion, and eagerness to share God's message of freedom in Him, to all open to receive it. Each decision we make carries its own set of consequences. I applaud your desire to spare others the needless pain, confusion, alienation, frustration, mental anguish, and slavery to the flesh that holds us captive when we make decisions outside of God's will. Your book will lead many on the path to receive healing, freedom, and forgiveness of self in the name of our Lord and Savior, Jesus Christ.

You've challenged your readers with thought-provoking questions to pursue a greater understanding of why we make the decisions we do. Thank you for your insight and your unique style of bringing the story of Ruth to life. At some point in each of our lives, our journey will inevitably thrust us into unknown territory. You have made it clear in your book that without God, we will definitely be derailed.

Is Your Name Orpah?

I'd have to say yes, at times, it has been. I could certainly see parallels in my own life with that of Orpah's. There have been times throughout my life where I've been at a crossroad and not known which way to turn. Orpah had to make a decision that would alter her life forever, "Do I stay or return home?" I've had periods of being indecisive out of fear of making the wrong decision. Perhaps Orpah struggled with that thought as she tried to make her decision. I have had my share of being a people pleaser at the cost of my own well-being. I've wanted to cling to the familiar and stay comfortable and safe within my own box. I've allowed my past pain to cripple my spirit and divert my focus away from God.

We don't know what kind of pain Orpah may have suffered as a result of her decision to return to Moab. However, I do know that we can often suffer unnecessary mental, emotional, and physical stress and pain when we allow ourselves to look back when we should be looking forward and UP! I have allowed my own pain to propel me to act in a manner completely out my character. I was holding onto a piece of my past that I should have let go of. My behavior brought humiliation, sadness, and overwhelming guilt because I did what I thought I needed to do instead of what God wanted me to do. My impatience to bring an end to my pain forced me to experience a major setback.

God always provides a way out when we are teetering on the fence of what's right or wrong. We have to be strong enough and well read enough to know what His promises are. (No temptation has seized you except what is common to man.) And God is faithful; He will not let you be tempted beyond what you can bear. But when you are tempted, He will also provide a way out so that you can stand up under it. (1 Corinthians 10:13)

Looking back and allowing our grief to consume us can rob us of the precious present.

Thank you for reminding us that we can experience a life-altering freedom when we surrender it all to God. You've made it crystal clear that the only way to go is God's way. It has taken me some time, growth, maturity, and faith to discover that in the midst of my deepest pain, birth is given to greater growth, strengthened faith, freedom, and peace that can only be granted by God Himself. We truly do serve an awesome God!

I find it easier to forgive others than I do myself. I know that we all fall short of the glory of God. I still struggle from time to time with unforgiveness of self, which leads me to dependence and resting assured that I have been forgiven by the One who created me and knows everything about me. *Ready to Change My Name* is on course and timely for anyone seeking forgiveness, peace, freedom, and a deeper relationship with Christ.

Don't Turn Back!

With God's love, grace, mercy, and guidance, I WON'T turn back! If God is for us, who can be against us?

Removal of the Masks

Thank you for taking off your mask and sharing your story in order to set us free. May we all remove the masks that keep us in bondage and hinder our growth toward God's desire to give us a hope and a future. I have slowly begun to shed my masks and not please people at the expense of my own well-being. We are instructed by God to love, support, and help each other. I had to realize that it's not selfish to take care of myself; it's absolutely necessary! We must take the time to nurture our minds, bodies, and souls first and bring them in alignment with the will of God before we offer real help to anyone. You graciously shared your experience with people pleasing. I used to be more concerned about people's opinions rather than God's. It is truly liberating to know that we are not subject to man's approval for validation. It's easy to lose sight of that fact in the world we live in. Our validation came from God Almighty the moment He created us.

The Transformation Begins

I've learned to stop torturing myself with self-doubt, unwarranted guilt, anxiety, feelings of inadequacy, and self-imposed fear. I'm much nicer to myself and have learned to embrace my mistakes as a part of the Master's plan. There are times that God allows us to fall to be humbled and broken to promote a greater understanding of what that feels like, so that we may empathize and bring comfort to someone else. "For just as the sufferings of Christ flow over into our lives, so also through Christ our comfort overflows." (2 Corinthians 1:5)

We are children of the King and our steps are ordered by Him! Through hardship, I have gained a greater appreciation for the calm before the storm. I am no longer trapped by the fear of adversity or pain because I know that growth, maturity, transformation, joy, peace, and freedom bloom after the storm is over!

From Darkness into the Light!

When we cross over from darkness into the light, we experience true deliverance. You've reminded us that we keep Satan at bay when we walk in the light! We are no longer suffocated by the vice grip of bondage to the flesh.

Healing in His Wings!

I unequivocally know, there <u>IS</u> Healing In His Wings!

May God continue to shower you with His blessings and keep you anchored in His Word. May God have favor upon you as you boldly and courageously share His Word!

Susan Mackey, Alpharetta, GA

Gail, I want to thank you. The first edition of *Ready to Change My Name* really touched me. I mean it really did. I thought I was looking at my life. I too had moved from Georgia and came back to Ohio for ministry reasons and it has been some mountain and valley experiences. I am encouraging my husband to read your book.

Reverend Nicole Colvin, Associate Pastor
Greater Mitchell Chapel AME, Mansfield, OH

I have read and reviewed *Ready to Change My Name*. I was delighted and hopeful at the relevance of this book for women who are at the crossroads of major decisions in their lives. I found it particularly helpful for women who are early in their recovery from bad relationships, and alcohol and other drug addictions.

Women in these traumatic situations desperately need the support, guidance, validation, and spiritual significance of this book. This book presents a step-by-step guide through which the reader is encouraged to move through the internal and external elements and obstacles that have prevented them from having a glorious relationship with Jesus Christ and all the wonderful gifts He is ready to bestow upon them if they only ask.

Although *Ready to Change My Name* is based on a biblical story of women, its application is also important for men as well who are struggling with issues in their lives. As the foreword indicates, "In this book are the very tools to help all people of faith realize their God-given potential by finding the courage to face themselves."

Sincerely and With God's Grace and Mercy in My Own Life,

Judy Wright
Everlasting ARM (Addiction Recovery Ministry) of
Mount Zion Baptist Church

YOUR STORY

My name is _____ and this is my story.

_____

_____

_____

_____

_____

_____

_____

_____

_____

_____

_____

_____

_____

_____

_____

_____

STEPS ON THE JOURNEY

30-DAY JOURNAL

Day One:

_____

_____

_____

_____

_____

_____

_____

_____

_____

_____

_____

_____

_____

_____

_____

_____

_____

_____

_____

_____

_____

_____

_____

_____

_____

_____

Day Two:

_____

_____

_____

_____

_____

_____

_____

_____

_____

_____

_____

_____

_____

_____

_____

_____

_____

_____

_____

_____

_____

_____

_____

_____

_____

_____

Day Three:

_____

_____

_____

_____

_____

_____

_____

_____

_____

_____

_____

_____

_____

_____

_____

_____

_____

_____

_____

_____

_____

_____

_____

_____

_____

Day Four:

_____

_____

_____

_____

_____

_____

_____

_____

_____

_____

_____

_____

_____

_____

_____

_____

_____

_____

_____

_____

_____

_____

_____

_____

_____

_____

_____

_____

Day Five:

_____

_____

_____

_____

_____

_____

_____

_____

_____

_____

_____

_____

_____

_____

_____

_____

_____

_____

_____

_____

_____

_____

_____

_____

_____

Day Six:

_____

_____

_____

_____

_____

_____

_____

_____

_____

_____

_____

_____

_____

_____

_____

_____

_____

_____

_____

_____

_____

_____

_____

_____

_____

_____

Day Seven:

_____

_____

_____

_____

_____

_____

_____

_____

_____

_____

_____

_____

_____

_____

_____

_____

_____

_____

_____

_____

_____

_____

_____

_____

_____

Day Eight:

_____

_____

_____

_____

_____

_____

_____

_____

_____

_____

_____

_____

_____

_____

_____

_____

_____

_____

_____

_____

_____

_____

_____

_____

_____

Day Nine:

_____

_____

_____

_____

_____

_____

_____

_____

_____

_____

_____

_____

_____

_____

_____

_____

_____

_____

_____

_____

_____

_____

_____

_____

_____

_____

Day Ten:

Day Eleven:

_____

_____

_____

_____

_____

_____

_____

_____

_____

_____

_____

_____

_____

_____

_____

_____

_____

_____

_____

_____

_____

_____

_____

_____

Day Twelve:

Day Thirteen:

_____

_____

_____

_____

_____

_____

_____

_____

_____

_____

_____

_____

_____

_____

_____

_____

_____

_____

_____

_____

_____

_____

_____

_____

Day Fourteen:

Day Fifteen:

_____

_____

_____

_____

_____

_____

_____

_____

_____

_____

_____

_____

_____

_____

_____

_____

_____

_____

_____

_____

_____

_____

_____

_____

Day Sixteen:

_____

_____

_____

_____

_____

_____

_____

_____

_____

_____

_____

_____

_____

_____

_____

_____

_____

_____

_____

_____

_____

_____

_____

_____

_____

_____

_____

Day Seventeen:

_____

_____

_____

_____

_____

_____

_____

_____

_____

_____

_____

_____

_____

_____

_____

_____

_____

_____

_____

_____

_____

_____

_____

_____

Day Eighteen:

Day Nineteen:

_____

_____

_____

_____

_____

_____

_____

_____

_____

_____

_____

_____

_____

_____

_____

_____

_____

_____

_____

_____

_____

_____

_____

_____

_____

Day Twenty:

Day Twenty-one:

_____

_____

_____

_____

_____

_____

_____

_____

_____

_____

_____

_____

_____

_____

_____

_____

_____

_____

_____

_____

_____

_____

_____

Day Twenty-two:

Day Twenty-three:

_____

_____

_____

_____

_____

_____

_____

_____

_____

_____

_____

_____

_____

_____

_____

_____

_____

_____

_____

_____

_____

_____

_____

_____

_____

_____

_____

_____

Day Twenty-four:

Day Twenty-five:

_____

_____

_____

_____

_____

_____

_____

_____

_____

_____

_____

_____

_____

_____

_____

_____

_____

_____

_____

_____

_____

_____

_____

_____

_____

Day Twenty-six:

Day Twenty-seven:

_____

_____

_____

_____

_____

_____

_____

_____

_____

_____

_____

_____

_____

_____

_____

_____

_____

_____

_____

_____

_____

_____

_____

_____

Day Twenty-eight:

_____

_____

_____

_____

_____

_____

_____

_____

_____

_____

_____

_____

_____

_____

_____

_____

_____

_____

_____

_____

_____

_____

_____

_____

_____

_____

_____

Day Twenty-nine:

_____

_____

_____

_____

_____

_____

_____

_____

_____

_____

_____

_____

_____

_____

_____

_____

_____

_____

_____

_____

_____

_____

_____

_____

_____

_____

Day Thirty:

And now, all glory to God, who is able to keep you from stumbling, and who will bring you into his glorious presence innocent of sin and with great joy. All glory to him, who alone is God our Savior, through Jesus Christ our Lord. Yes, glory, majesty, power, and authority belong to him, in the beginning, now, and forevermore. Amen.

Jude 24-26, NLT

A Final Thought

The end of our time together has come, but the next phase of your journey has only begun. I am excited about what the Lord is going to do. In the course of writing this book, I am constantly reminded that living our lives with God is greater than anything — even more than we can imagine. My own commitment in God has been strengthened, refined, and enhanced. Like you, I have a lot of work ahead of me and I'm ready to get started. No matter what you are going through right now, know that God is a good God and He can do anything but fail — especially for those who trust in Him. God has a wonderful plan for both you and me, and I pray that as we are transformed and grow into great women of God, we will embrace the process with great joy and peace. Please write me to share your personal testimonies, comments, words of encouragement, or to simply pray.

Ministry In Motion
Pastor Gail E. Dudley
5550 Cleveland Avenue
Columbus, OH 43231-4049
614-441-8178
www.GailDudley.com

SISTERS OF WISDOM
BOOK REVIEWS

"*Ready To Change My Name* can be the lever with which you can truly change your life. Profound and powerful, this book teaches us to remove our masks and not to turn back, which is at the very heart of our Christian life. I can't think of anyone who wouldn't be helped by reading this book and completing the 30-Day Journal. To God be the Glory for the many gifts He has given to Minister Gail."

Alyce M. Horton, Grafton, OH
Sisters of Wisdom Fellowship

"Minister Gail has the anointing of the Holy Spirit. Using the story of Naomi and her two daughters-in-law, Minister Gail focused on the one rarely mentioned: Orpah. Orpah was the one who turned back, did not take the risk, was clinging to her own fleshly concerns, and possibly missed what God had in store for her. This book is a MUST READ!"

Patricia Knight, Intercessory Prayer Warrior

"Minister Gail has a God-given gift to use plain and simple language to get her point across—a language that everyone can understand. This book challenges us to take off our masks, to face the unknown, to depend on God the Father, and to seek the face of the Living God. This book is a MUST READ for women and men alike."

Brenda A. Randleman
Ministry of Ruth

STATEMENT OF FAITH

GOD

We believe in one God, existing as three persons; Father, Son, and Holy Spirit, is the loving Creator of all that is, eternal and good, knowing all things, having all power, and desiring and inviting covenant relationship with humanity *(Matt. 28:19; 1 Tim. 1:17; Heb. 1:1-3; 9:14)*.

JESUS CHRIST

We believe in our Lord Jesus Christ, God manifest in the flesh. He alone is the Savior and Lord, the Son of God and God the Son, born of a virgin, the perfect example of humanity, crucified for the sin of the world, raised on the third day and who lives forever to make intercession for us. We confess the absolute lordship and leadership of the risen Jesus Christ, who is the Son of God and God the Son, and our soon-returning King *(Col. 1:15-20; Col. 2:9; John 1:1; Gal. 4:4; Phil. 3:10)*.

THE HOLY SPIRIT

We believe in God the Holy Spirit. At the point of salvation a person receives the Holy Spirit. We receive the abiding presence, peace, and power of the Holy Spirit in every believer as sufficient and necessary for normal Christian living *(Acts 1:8; Eph. 2:22; Rom. 8:9-30)*.

SCRIPTURE

We believe in the Holy Scripture as originally given by Christ, divinely inspired, and revealed by God, unchanging and infallible Word of God, correct doctrine, the complete truth, authority, and relevance of every promise, provision, God's story of love and redemption (John 1:1; 2 Pet. 1:19-21; 2 Tim. 2:15; 3:16).

SALVATION

We believe in the salvation of the lost and sinful people by grace alone, through faith alone, in Christ alone. We accept the grace of God through the finished work of Jesus on the cross as victory for eternal and abundant life, and we maintain spiritual sonship and citizenship in the present and future Kingdom of God *(Rom. 10:9-10; Eph. 2:8-9)*.

UNITY of THE BODY OF CHRIST

We believe in the unity of the Body of Christ and in the Spirit. Unity comprised of, teaching, prayer, fellowship, breaking of bread, meeting ministry needs, praise and worship, people being saved *(Eph. 4:1-6; Acts 2:42-47).*

HUMANITY

We celebrate the sacredness and uniqueness of every person as wonderfully created in the image of God and according to God's sovereign will, called to lives of Christlikeness through personal holiness, honor, and humility *(Heb. 2:6-12).*

SIN and EVIL

We acknowledge our sin and brokenness but refute anything that seeks to deny, discourage, or destroy the life that Jesus offers to all believers *(2 Cor. 4:1-18).*

MINISTRY

We believe that we should go, preach, and make disciples of Jesus Christ. We believe that we should be a witness for the Lord. We value the fellowship of Christian believers in loving community, gifted service, mutual encouragement and with godly leadership as representative of the presence of Christ on earth to meet the real needs of people *(Matt. 28:19-20; Acts 1:8; Acts 2:41-47).*

WORSHIP

We affirm that every person is called to glorify the living God completely, freely, and passionately by giving their lives in authentic relationship, their resources in responsible stewardship, and their devotion in faithful discipleship *(Jn. 4:23-24)*.

PRAYER

We believe in communication with God and availability to God to do God's will in the earth. We believe that we must go to God with our heart and come away with His *(Matt.6)*.

ABOUT THE AUTHOR

Gail E. Dudley

"...bringing you closer to Christ."

With a commitment to delivering messages that are both scriptural and applicable to real life situations, Gail E. Dudley shares the words that are spoken into her heart by the Holy Spirit and delivers those messages to the listener's ear.

One of her most rewarding experiences was participating as a conference speaker in Bulawayo, Zimbabwe, Africa, for The Women Unlimited of Word of Life International Annual Conference. Gail serves as a speaker and author with a passion to provide guidance to God's people as they navigate through their spiritual journey.

Currently Gail serves as a pastor at The Church at North Pointe, providing guidance, teaching discipleship studies, and overseeing multiple outreach efforts. She is also the Vice President of Diversity for Stonecroft Ministries, and works actively with the Mission America Coalition.

Gail is the wife of Reverend Dr. Kevin Dudley, senior pastor of The Church at North Pointe (Columbus, Ohio) and the loving mother of Alexander and Dominiq. Gail connects with people where they are in their journey and, upon hearing her speak, it is evident that Gail walks closely with the Lord, spends time daily in the Word, and seeks always to be ready to share God's truth for transforming lives.

BOOKING INFORMATION

If you would like to schedule Gail to speak at your retreat, your book club, or to do a book signing or a reading, please contact, Gail at:

www.GailDudley.com
GED@MIMToday.org
614-441-8178

We would love to hear from you. Send us your testimony and/or prayer request.

Transformational Weekend Retreats

In our culture today believers inevitably find themselves living their lives based upon false beliefs, very often unaware of the many harmful influences that have shaped and continue to hold us captive. To experience a life of truth it is absolutely critical to know the truth. God's truth is what sets us free! Many people have the desire to know the truth, but are unsure how to connect and apply God's truth. Just as we do today, the woman in Genesis 3 fell into the serpent's trap, but God gives us all that we need to overcome the lies. During this transformational weekend participants will gain insight that will help to strengthen and inspire us in our walk with the Lord.

If you desire to go deeper in your walk with Christ, this is for you.

We will start each "Transformational Weekend" on the scheduled Friday at 6:00 p.m. in a time of prayer instruction and inner healing followed by quiet time. Saturday morning beginning at 9:30 we will identify the lies that have been spoken into our life and replace those lies with the truth by asking, "Who Told You That?" The second session on Saturday, "Ready to Change My Name," will position us for transformation.

Our weekend will conclude at 3:00 p.m. with small group instruction that will equip each participant to form small groups and share this teaching with others.

Space is limited. Only twelve participants per scheduled weekend retreat. Cost: $125.00 per person ~ includes all sessions and materials. Interesting in learning more about the "Transformational Weekend Retreats?" Want to place yourself on the upcoming retreat list? Contact: GED@MIMToday.org

OTHER BOOKS BY GAIL

Ready to Change My Name ~
A Spiritual Journey from Fear to Faith

Ready to Pray Workbook ~
A Spiritual Journey of Praise and Worship

Ready to Pray (30 Minute Prayer CD)

Transparent Moments of Gail Dudley

Who Told You That? ~
The Truth Behind the Lies

ORDER ADDITIONAL COPIES TODAY

Gail E. Dudley
5550 Cleveland Avenue
Columbus, Ohio 43231-4049

Name: _____

Address: _____

City: _____ State: _____ Zip: _____

E-mail: _____

Would you like to join our mailing list? ❑ Yes   ❑ No thank you.

Telephone: (___) _____ - _____

Ready to Change My Name	qty: _____	($15.00 each + $2.50 S & H)
Ready to Pray (the Book)	qty: _____	($15.00 each + $2.50 S & H)
Ready to Pray (215-page Workbook)	qty: _____	($24.95 each + $3.50 S & H)
Ready to Pray (30 Minute Prayer CD)	qty: _____	($7.00 each + $2.50 S & H)
Who Told You That?	qty: _____	($17.50 each + $3.00 S & H)
Transparent Moments	qty: _____	($7.00 each + $3.00 S & H)

Book Total: $ _____   S & H Total: _____ = Grand Total $_____

Number of books being shipped: _____

Please make checks payable to:
Gail E. Dudley

Send payment to:
5550 Cleveland Avenue, Columbus, Ohio 43231-4049

Please allow two (2) weeks for shipping

CPSIA information can be obtained at www.ICGtesting.com
Printed in the USA
BVOW04s0737030415

394543BV00007B/173/P